To Drown Hell and Burn Heaven

*Cycle A Sermons for
Proper 15 Through Proper 23
Based on the Gospel Texts*

Kristin Borsgard Wee

CSS Publishing Company, Inc.
Lima, Ohio

TO DROWN HELL AND BURN HEAVEN

FIRST EDITION
Copyright © 2013
by CSS Publishing Co., Inc.

Published by CSS Publishing Company, Inc., Lima, Ohio 45807. All rights reserved. No part of this publication may be reproduced in any manner whatsoever without the prior permission of the publisher, except in the case of brief quotations embodied in critical articles and reviews. Inquiries should be addressed to: CSS Publishing Company, Inc., Permissions Department, 5450 N. Dixie Highway, Lima, Ohio 45807.

Scripture quotations are from the New Revised Standard Version of the Bible. Copyright 1989 by the Division of Christian Education of the National Council of the Churches of Christ in the USA, Nashville, Thomas Nelson Publishers © 1989. Used by permission. All rights reserved.

Library of Congress Cataloging-in-Publication Data
Wee, Kristin Borsgard, 1942-
    To drown hell and burn heaven : Cycle A sermons for proper 15 through proper 23 based on the gospel texts / Kristin Wee. -- FIRST EDITION.
       pages cm
    ISBN 0-7880-2712-3 (alk. paper)
    1. Bible. N.T. Matthew--Sermons. 2. Pentecost season--Sermons. 3. Common lectionary (1992) I. Title.

    BS2575.54.W44 2013
    252'.64--dc23
                         2013010306

For more information about CSS Publishing Company resources, visit our website at www.csspub.com, email us at csr@csspub.com, or call (800) 241-4056.

ISBN-13: 978-0-7880-2712-3
ISBN-10: 0-7880-2712-3   PRINTED IN USA

*For my children, Marit, Astri, Tryg, and Britta.
You give me energy for living and hope for the future.*

Table of Contents

Introduction   7

Proper 15   9
Pentecost 13
Ordinary Time 20
   Matthew 15:21-28
   An Uppity Woman

Proper 16   13
Pentecost 14
Ordinary Time 21
   Matthew 16:13-20
   Some Enchanted Evening

Proper 17   17
Pentecost 15
Ordinary Time 22
   Matthew 16:21-28
   Smother Love

Proper 18   21
Pentecost 16
Ordinary Time 23
   Matthew 18:15-20
   Rat Poison

Proper 18 — Alternative Sermon   25
   Matthew 18:15-20
   Stopping the Spread of Hell

Proper 19   31
Pentecost 17
Ordinary Time 24
   Matthew 18:21-35
   Throwing Away the Calculator

Proper 20   35
Pentecost 18
Ordinary Time 25
   Matthew 20:1-16
   To Drown Hell and Burn Heaven

Proper 20 — Alternative Sermon   41
   Matthew 20:1-16
   Being Too Generous

Proper 21   45
Pentecost 19
Ordinary Time 26
   Matthew 21:23-32
   The Gift of Failure

Proper 22   49
Pentecost 20
Ordinary Time 27
   Matthew 21:33-46
   Divine Tenants

Proper 22 — Alternative Sermon   53
   Matthew 21:33-46
   Captains or Parties

Proper 23   59
Pentecost 21
Ordinary Time 28
   Matthew 22:1-14
   Wedding Guests

If You Like This Book...   63

Introduction

Church

I will never forget the World's Fair the summer of 1965. It was the first time I saw Michelangelo's *Pieta*. I burst into tears. That image, for me, contained all of the others: the precocious little boy with the skinned knees, the bright teenager testing parental limits, the brave prophetic preacher, the teacher who raised more questions than he answered, a friend who instinctively understood group dynamics, encourager-challenger, feeder-healer-forgiver, a man who with grace and dignity died a death that was intended to be demeaning; then shocked everyone by defeating death. His life was about salvation as much as his death was. The church embodies all of this as Christ's living presence here as it prays for peace and works for justice, giving birth over and over to the love with which Jesus loved his world, and living the divine life now that is also waiting for us at the end of this one.

Why I Write

As a pastor and disciple of Jesus, I sometimes have the privilege of witnessing the power of the Spirit to inspire a person's imagination in a way that creates new life. When that happens, people often find themselves envisioning new images for their lives, their neighbors, their relationships, and may even see their world in a new way through unveiled eyes. Words have power to effect that change. Like an old woman with cataracts is drawn to the light, I am drawn not just to the written word but to what is there between the lines, what the rabbis referred to as the "white fire" that is happening between every two words of Torah. The words themselves almost have their own souls as we struggle to write them, say them, and be led by them. They seem to take on a life of their own. They strain to bear holy realities and experiences of grace for which words are always inadequate.

But words do have the ability to comfort, heal, bless, and make alive. Words may even question our domesticated version of God, causing us to wonder whether the God we know is the God who is. Grappling with the words of scripture and the words I use to describe the mystery captured there means that I must first take them into myself and grapple with what they mean for my life, decisions, and relationships before I attempt to put them at the disposal of others for theirs. I know that words are not meant to stay on a page but to fly off the page and into our hearts and through our imaginations into the hearts of others. I am a sucker for a challenge, and this — in my opinion — is one that beats most of the others cold.

Proper 15
Pentecost 13
Ordinary Time 20
Matthew 15:21-28

An Uppity Woman

> Jesus left that place and went away to the district of Tyre and Sidon. Just then a Canaanite woman from that region came out and started shouting, "Have mercy on me, Lord, Son of David; my daughter is tormented by a demon." But he did not answer her at all. And his disciples came and urged him, saying, "Send her away, for she keeps shouting after us." He answered, "I was sent only to the lost sheep of the house of Israel." But she came and knelt before him, saying, "Lord, help me." He answered, "It is not fair to take the children's food and throw it to the dogs." She said, "Yes, Lord, yet even the dogs eat the crumbs that fall from their masters' table." Then Jesus answered her, "Woman, great is your faith! Let it be done for you as you wish." And her daughter was healed instantly.

When I was a kid, we played a game in which we would stare into each others eyes until one gave in and blinked. We used tricks to win sometimes, but above all we would refuse to back down no matter how much our eyes were hurting. Something like that is going on between Jesus and the Canaanite woman.

There is a stand-off happening here. I think it is helpful to know that Jesus has just gone through a difficult time. He recently learned of the beheading of his cousin, John the Baptist. Jesus tries to withdraw from the crowds of people who were following him, but they won't let him escape. He ends up feeding thousands with a few loaves of bread and a couple of fish. Then there is a storm at sea and Peter's walking on the water, which is sabotaged by his fear and doubt. Everywhere Jesus looks he finds people who want what he can do for them but who remain blind to who he is. He is tired and at the end of his rope.

Then a foreign woman shows up, one more person with needs, and Jesus draws the line. Enough is enough. He's tired and cranky, so he rudely dismisses her. But she will not stay on her side of the line. Doesn't she get it? Can't she hear? The man said "no." But she doesn't budge, even when Jesus calls her a dog. When she answers that even dogs get the crumbs, something in Jesus snaps. He blinks... his anger dissolves... and something inside of him is forever changed. You can hear it in his voice: "O woman, great is your faith. Let it be done for you as you wish" (v. 28). Her daughter is healed instantly. Through her faith, Jesus learns that God's plan for him is bigger than he had imagined. She was bright and uppity and faithful, and she refused to stay behind the line.

Dorothy Day was like that too. It was her vocation to love the poor and care for people who slept in doorways. Dorothy Day and Peter Maurin founded the Catholic Worker Society in 1932. Dorothy met a lot of opposition, but she continued to love those that others couldn't bring themselves to love. Some would have called her an uppity woman. Her work among the poor grew to enormous proportions and the *Catholic Worker* newspaper spread throughout the world. One man, tossing in an uncomfortable bed in the state of Sonora in Mexico got up to turn over the mattress. Underneath he found a copy of the *Catholic Worker*. A miner once found a copy five miles underground in an old mine under the Atlantic Ocean off Nova Scotia. A seminarian in Rome sent out his shoes to have new soles put on them. They came back to him wrapped in a copy of the *Catholic Worker*. Dorothy Day was a determined woman who owned nothing herself, choosing to live with the poverty of the people that she served. What she started spread throughout the world. She was a person who refused to toe the line society had drawn for her.

Saint Teresa was another uppity woman. Back in the sixteenth century Teresa joined the Carmelite order of nuns. Once she was in the cloister, she saw the need for reform. The Carmelite nuns of her time lived in great luxury without much practice of the Christian faith. Teresa began a massive reform. She established seventeen new convents in Spain. The Vatican made fun of her and said, "She was proud and disobedient and teaches theology as though she were a doctor of the church." In 1970, four centuries later, the Roman Catholic church proclaimed Saint Teresa a "Doctor of the Church." Teresa was definitely an uppity woman.

Then there was Simone Weil. She was a French school teacher and philosopher who died in 1943 at the age of 34. She was also a woman with a conscience. Born to wealthy Jewish parents, Simone at a very early age began to show compassion for those who suffered. At the age of five she refused to eat sugar. The soldiers who were fighting the war didn't have any, so she felt it wasn't right for her to have it either. Later in life she decided not to wear socks because the children of workers went without them. She identified with people who suffered from war, hunger, unemployment, or anything that keeps people from being free. Simone Weil wrote these words: "The love of our neighbor in all its fullness simply means being able to say to him or her, 'What are you going through?' " Some probably thought of her as an uppity woman.

All four of these women had something in common. They swam against the tide. They were women of courage who refused to stay on their side of the line society had drawn. They argued with conviction. They were women of faith. They knew that God could show up anywhere, even on the far side of the lines we draw to protect ourselves. So the lesson for us is to let go. Step out. Look a Canaanite in the eye, knock on a strange door, talk to an outsider, take a risk, push a limit. God is at work rubbing out the lines we draw and calling us into a love without limits. Sometimes humility is not in order... and being uppity is. Amen.

Proper 16
Pentecost 14
Ordinary Time 21
Matthew 16:13-20

Some Enchanted Evening

> Now when Jesus came into the district of Caesarea Philippi, he asked his disciples, "Who do people say that the Son of Man is?" And they said, "Some say John the Baptist, but others Elijah, and still others Jeremiah or one of the prophets." He said to them, "But who do you say that I am?" Simon Peter answered, "You are the Messiah, the Son of the living God." And Jesus answered him, "Blessed are you, Simon son of Jonah! For flesh and blood has not revealed this to you, but my Father in heaven. And I tell you, you are Peter, and on this rock I will build my church, and the gates of Hades will not prevail against it. I will give you the keys of the kingdom of heaven, and whatever you bind on earth will be bound in heaven, and whatever you loose on earth will be loosed in heaven." Then he sternly ordered the disciples not to tell anyone that he was the Messiah.

Last summer, a large crowd gathered at the Wee family cabin in northern Minnesota to celebrate my mother-in-law's ninetieth birthday. At one point I realized that all the relatives had gone outside and I was in the middle of a room full of strangers. It's an awkward feeling. I wished that someone would come in who would be happy to see me and make their way toward me through that crowd of strangers.

A similar thought is expressed in an old song, "Some Enchanted Evening."

> Some enchanted evening
> You will see a stranger,
> You will see a stranger

> Across a crowded room.
> And somehow you'll know,
> You'll know even then
> That somewhere you'll see him
> Again and again.[1]

Just for a few minutes, imagine Jesus in that role. Imagine that Jesus is on the far side of a crowded room full of strangers. He catches your eye. He is happy to see you and begins to edge his way through the crowd toward you. But there is a question on his face. As he slowly comes toward you, his eyes intent on you, it dawns on you what the question is. He is coming to ask *you* the same question he asked of his disciples that day, "Who do *you* say that I am?"

Your adrenalin kicks in, your hands start to sweat, and your heart speeds up. "Oh my goodness," you think. "It's really Jesus. He's actually here." Your mind goes through some nervous flashbacks to confirmation classes and Sunday sermons and Bible studies and all the things you learned about Jesus. What *did* you learn? Is there a right answer to the question, "Who is Jesus?"

As he continues to come in your direction, the butterflies become more active in your stomach. You remember the conversation between Jesus and the disciples. Jesus asks them what people are saying about who he is, and the disciples answer him by saying, "Well, some say you are John the Baptist, others say you are Elijah, and still others say one of the prophets."

But, that's what *other* people were saying. Then Jesus gets specific, "But, who do *you* say that I am?" he asked the disciples. Now you have to decide how you will answer that question. Jesus is coming closer. What will you say?

As you think back to what you learned about him, you remember that the reaction to him was mixed. There were people who loved him and people who hated him. Some expected him to be a great warrior king like David or a great prophet like Elijah. Whatever he was, he would be called "Wonderful Counselor, Mighty God, Everlasting Father, Prince of Peace" (Isaiah 9:6b), and his kingdom would prosper and peace would be endless.

But he wasn't a king or a priest or a prophet and some of his best friends were prostitutes and crooks. Who is this man? Jesus is coming closer. His eyes shine with love as he smiles at you, but the question is there on his face. How are you going to answer him?

You remember learning in confirmation that Moses was the great leader of the Old Testament. Moses was, but Jesus claimed to be a higher authority. Moses was against murder. Jesus was against vindictive anger. Moses was against adultery. Jesus was against recreational sex. Moses said love your neighbor. Jesus said love your enemy too. Moses said be good. Jesus said be perfect. Who did he think he was, anyway? Who can be perfect? Who even wants to try?

The thought flickers through your mind that you could ask Jesus who *he* says he is. But you dismiss that crazy idea almost as fast as it appears. He's almost here.

You remember that his followers attributed a great many miracles to him. He even brought a dead person back to life. But there was one miracle he couldn't pull off and that was saving his own skin. He died just as dead on the cross as all the others before him. His followers say he rose from the dead, but the world is in just as bad shape now as it was then, maybe worse. So what difference does he make? Now there are only a small handful of people between Jesus and you. You'll have to answer that question very soon.

Then it hits you. Your discovery of who he is must be just that, *your* discovery. It must be a personal definition. It all boils down to "What do *you* say?" Jesus wants to know what *you* say and what *you* think. It occurs to you that Christianity isn't knowing about Jesus so much as it is knowing

Jesus. Jesus just has two more people to pass and then he will be standing before you. The love and the question are mingled together on his face.

Frantically your mind is churning. You remember some lines from Ann Lamott. In the midst of her addictions, she was struggling to define who Jesus was for her. She asked a friend what it meant for him that he was "saved." He answered her, "I guess it's like discovering you're on the shelf of a pawnshop, dusty and forgotten and maybe not worth very much. Then Jesus comes in and tells the pawnbroker, 'I'll take her place on the shelf. Let her go outside again.'"

The time is up. Jesus stands before you. Your heart is pounding. He looks at you as if he really knows you. The love in his eyes is radiant and then he says the words you know he will say, "Who do *you* say that I am?" "Who am I to *you*?" The breath catches in your throat. Your life seems to hang in the balance. The enchanted evening of the song has happened only the stranger isn't a stranger at all, it is Jesus. How will you answer him? Amen.

---

1. "Some Enchanted Evening" copyright © 1949 by Richard Rodgers and Oscar Hammerstein II. Copyright Renewed Williamson Music (ASCAP), an Imagem Company, owner of publication and allied rights throughout the World. International copyright secured. All rights reserved. Used by permission.

Proper 17
Pentecost 15
Ordinary Time 22
Matthew 16:21-28

Smother Love

From that time on, Jesus began to show his disciples that he must go to Jerusalem and undergo great suffering at the hands of the elders and chief priests and scribes, and be killed, and on the third day be raised. And Peter took him aside and began to rebuke him, saying, "God forbid it, Lord! This must never happen to you." But he turned and said to Peter, "Get behind me, Satan! You are a stumbling block to me; for you are setting your mind not on divine things but on human things." Then Jesus told his disciples, "If any want to become my followers, let them deny themselves and take up their cross and follow me. For those who want to save their life will lose it, and those who lose their life for my sake will find it. For what will it profit them if they gain the whole world but forfeit their life? Or what will they give in return for their life? For the Son of Man is to come with his angels in the glory of his Father, and then he will repay everyone for what has been done. Truly I tell you, there are some standing here who will not taste death before they see the Son of Man coming in his kingdom."

I loved my father very much. He was my security, my hero, my knight in shining armor. But he wasn't perfect.

My dad had "a plan" for each of us three kids. We were supposed to go off to college, and then come back home to teach school, preferably in the same school where my dad taught. My older brother functioned pretty much according to plan. I didn't. After college I made plans to go to graduate school in New York City. All summer I was telling my parents how excited I was about going to New York. On the day I was to leave, I piled up my luggage in the middle of the living room floor, then sat down to wait for my friend to pick me up. My father put his newspaper down and said, "So, what are your plans for the fall, Kris?" I was shocked. "What are my plans?" I repeated like a parrot. I couldn't believe my ears. My luggage was right there in front of him. Hadn't he heard me at all? I realized then how much he did not want me to go. He wanted me to stay home with him.

Smother love is common in our society. We see it in parents who do not put limits on their children. We see it in the husband who loves his wife so much he does everything for her, so she becomes helpless when he dies. We see it in the mother who ties her daughter to herself with invisible apron strings, and that mother would be shocked if someone called her a devil. But that's what Jesus called Peter. "Get behind me, Satan!" Jesus said. "You are a stumbling block to me" (v. 23). Peter was using smother love on Jesus. He wasn't being mean or careless. Just the opposite. When he heard that Jesus was going to suffer, Peter said, "God forbid." Peter couldn't stand the thought that Jesus would be hurt or killed. All Peter says is "God forbid," and Jesus explodes. What did Peter do that was so wrong? By suggesting there had to be a better plan, Peter was simply saying what most of us would have said.

But as far as Jesus was concerned, it was Satan talking. From the beginning of time, Satan has offered the easy way out — an alternative to God's way. For Jesus it must have been tempting to play it safe, to skip the trip to Jerusalem and find another way to save the world. If it hadn't been tempting, he probably wouldn't have reacted to Peter so harshly.

There's another problem here. Jesus says he must be ready to suffer and die. Is he expecting us to do the same? That's alarming. I want to believe that God *gives* me my life, not that God wants to take it away. I can't imagine that God is looking forward to my funeral. Doesn't God want me to be happy and comfortable and safe?

This gospel text answers a resounding "No!" What God cares about is not my happiness or my comfort. What God is really interested in is the *quality* of my life. God isn't just concerned with the health of my body or the state of my mind. God is passionate about the depth of my life, the scope and zest of all that motivates and sustains me. Fear of death can turn into fear of life, making us live in a cautious, stingy way that isn't life at all. According to Jesus, the way to have abundant life is not to save it but to spend it.

There was a man who understood that completely. Listen to these words from Count Von Moltke. He wrote them in a letter to his wife from a prison in Nazi Germany in January of 1945. Von Moltke had been arrested and condemned to death, not because he conspired against Hitler, but because he had warned a friend that he was going to be arrested. Von Moltke wrote these words to his wife the day before he was to die.

> Dear heart: First I must tell you that quite evidently the last 24 hours of one's life are no different from any others. I had always imagined that it would come as a shock to say to oneself: "Now the sun is setting for the last time for you, now the hour hand will make only two more revolutions before 12, now you are going to bed for the last time." Nothing of the sort. Perhaps I am a little cracked. For I cannot deny that I am in really high spirits. I only pray to God in heaven to sustain me in this mood, for surely it is easier for the flesh to die in this state. How merciful the Lord has been to me! In the courtroom, when I was called up for my last words, I was in such a frame of mind that I nearly said, "I have only one thing to add to my defense. Take my goods, my honour, my children, and wife; the body they may kill; God's truth abideth still, his kingdom is forever."
> Just a moment ago I cried a little, not sadly, not pensively, not because I want to go back, but out of gratitude and awe at this documentation on the part of God. It is not granted us to see him face-to-face, but we cannot but be overawed when suddenly we recognize that throughout life he has gone before us

as a cloud by day and as a pillar of fire by night, and that he is allowing us suddenly, in a single instant, to perceive this. Now nothing further can happen. Dear heart, my life is finished, and I can say of myself: "He died old and sated with life." (He was 38 years old.) But that doesn't alter the fact that I would like to live a little longer, that I should like to accompany you a little further on this earth. But that would require a new mission from God. The mission for which God made me is fulfilled. All our beloved sayings are in my heart and in your heart. But by virtue of the treasure that has spoken through me and that fills this humble earthen vessel, I say to you in concluding: The grace of the Lord Jesus Christ, and the love of God, and the communion of the Holy Ghost be with you all. Amen.[1]

Living in faith is about living a life that matters — a life lived for Christ's sake. When we do that, we can say, "Take my goods, my honor, my children, my wife, the body they may kill; God's truth abideth still. His kingdom is forever." Amen.

---

1. Helmut Gollwitzer and Kathe Kuhn editors, *Dying We Live* (New York: Pantheon Books Inc., 1956), p. 123.

Proper 18
Pentecost 16
Ordinary Time 23
Matthew 18:15-20

Rat Poison

If another member of the church sins against you, go and point out the fault when the two of you are alone. If the member listens to you, you have regained that one. But if you are not listened to, take one or two others along with you, so that every word may be confirmed by the evidence of two or three witnesses. If the member refuses to listen to them, tell it to the church; and if the offender refuses to listen even to the church, let such a one be to you as a Gentile and a tax collector. Truly I tell you, whatever you bind on earth will be bound in heaven, and whatever you loose on earth will be loosed in heaven. Again, truly I tell you, if two of you agree on earth about anything you ask, it will be done for you by my Father in heaven. For where two or three are gathered in my name, I am there among them.

When our son started kindergarten, I held my breath. I knew he would be a handful. Things were going along pretty well until the day he pulled the fire alarm, which he did during lunch hour. The whole school was in chaos. I got a vivid description from the principal. I felt awful. I'll always be grateful to the teacher who said that my son was not a bad kid and I shouldn't let the principal convince me any differently. But not so from my son's teacher. She had nothing good to say about him. But then, she had nothing good to say about the other students either. That was when I began to get suspicious. I was more suspicious when my son began to bring his work home with sad faces stamped on them. He was learning the letter "B." One of his papers was a drawing of a tree with a lot of hidden letter *B*s. He had found fourteen of the fifteen *B*s, but the teacher had stamped sad faces all over the page. Happy face stamps I had seen. I didn't even know a sad face stamp existed. Until then. She stamped them all over my son's papers like she was testing out new ink pads. I daydreamed about sneaking into her classroom in the middle of the night. I would destroy that sad face stamp and replace it with ten dozen happy face stamps. My anger continued to grow.

Matthew's words are directed at people like me. Often, when I am angry, I can take a step back to look for the cause of the problem within myself and see that I am in some way responsible for the situation and do something to change it. When my anger goes on and on then it is not just plain anger anymore. It becomes bitterness or resentment. Someone called it "arthritis of the spirit." There is some real motivation for learning how to deal with this problem. We owe it to God, we owe it to the community, and we owe it to ourselves.

Because, you see, resentment deforms us. We use our resentment to hurt someone else before they can hurt us again. Before we know it, it has begun to poison us. Anne Lamott says, "Not forgiving is like drinking rat poison and then waiting for the rat to die." Isn't that the truth? Who do we think we are hurting with our angry, bitter, unforgiving thoughts… someone else? No. We are hurting ourselves. Barbara Brown Taylor says this resentment is like a boomerang. We use it to protect ourselves — to hurt someone else — but it has a sinister way of circling right back at us so that we become the victim of our own poisonous feelings.

Mary Gordon wrote an essay on anger for the *New York Times*. One hot August afternoon, she was in the kitchen preparing dinner for ten. Although the house was full of people, no one offered to help her with the chopping, mixing, and setting the table. She was stewing in her own juices. Then her

78-year-old mother and her two small children insisted that she stop what she was doing and take them swimming. They went out and got in the car. They started leaning on the horn and shouting out the windows so all the neighbors could hear them. They were loudly reminding her that she had promised to take them swimming. That, says Gordon, was when she lost it. She flew outside and jumped on the hood of the car. She pounded on the windshield. She told her mother and her children that she was never, ever going to take any of them anywhere again and none of them would ever be permitted to have one friend in any house of hers until the hour of their death which, she said, she hoped would be soon.

Then the frightening thing happened. Gordon says, "I became a huge bird. A carrion crow. My legs became hard stalks, my eyes were sharp and vicious. I developed a murderous beak. Greasy black feathers took the place of arms. I flapped and flapped. I blotted out the sun's light with my flapping." Even after she had been forced off the hood of the car, it took a while to come back to herself. When she did, she was appalled, because she realized she had genuinely frightened her children. Her son said to her, "I was scared because I didn't know who you were." Gordon concludes that "sin makes the sinner unrecognizable." The only antidote is forgiveness.[1]

Here in Matthew, Jesus lays out a formula for dealing with conflict. Immediately following this reading are the words about forgiving seventy times seven. It's no accident. Jesus wants to protect the community. He wants to keep it — and us — from being fractured by our anger, from being poisoned.

I finally screwed up my courage and went to talk to that teacher. I really didn't like her. Her skirts were too short, her make-up too thick, and she was bossy and opinionated. But I stated my case with as much kindness as I could muster. As we talked, I began to see things I hadn't seen before. She told me she had suffered a series of miscarriages and might not be able to have a child. Her husband lost his job and suddenly the veil dropped. I felt my poison begin to dissipate. I was so consumed by my anger that I didn't really see her or her feelings. I began to feel the waters of grace flowing over me and the wind of the spirit of forgiveness blowing through my bones. My voice became kinder. I still didn't really like her, and I didn't think she was a good teacher, but something changed when I saw that she was scared and hurt and vulnerable.

When we allow our enemy to stop being our enemy, the rules change. Nobody knows how to act anymore. It is a quiet revolution like a fist slowly uncurling. What we gain is the chance to live again, free from the poison that has been killing us. God knows we need lots of practice in the process of reconciliation and forgiveness. So God gives us the ultimate in assistance. Jesus said, "Where two or three are gathered in my name, I am there" (v. 20). He covers us with a waterfall of forgiveness and then promises to be there with us when we take this messy business in hand. A wise man once said, "The person who cannot reconcile, breaks the bridge over which he himself must pass." Let's change that statement a little. The Christian who *can* reconcile, not only crosses the bridge to a new life, but the poison stops, and Jesus crosses with him. Amen.

---

1. Mary Gordon, *New York Times*, June 13, 1993.

Alternative Sermon for

Proper 18
Pentecost 16
Ordinary Time 23
Matthew 18:15-20

Stopping the Spread of Hell

> If another member of the church sins against you, go and point out the fault when the two of you are alone. If the member listens to you, you have regained that one. But if you are not listened to, take one or two others along with you, so that every word may be confirmed by the evidence of two or three witnesses. If the member refuses to listen to them, tell it to the church; and if the offender refuses to listen even to the church, let such a one be to you as a Gentile and a tax collector. Truly I tell you, whatever you bind on earth will be bound in heaven, and whatever you loose on earth will be loosed in heaven. Again, truly I tell you, if two of you agree on earth about anything you ask, it will be done for you by my Father in heaven. For where two or three are gathered in my name, I am there among them.

A month ago I had a conversation with a clerk in a store on Main Street. She told me she had had an argument with a pastor years ago and got so angry she never went back to church. She said, "Don't you think I can be just as good a Christian communing with God in the beauty of my backyard as I can be if I were going to church?" I took a deep breath and said, "No. I don't. I'm not at all sure that we can be God's people without putting ourselves in the midst of God's people. I need those other people to learn with, to give and receive help, and to be my extended family." She said, "Well I sure don't need them. I'm a private Christian."

Here in Matthew Jesus says faith is not a private matter. Jesus promised to be in our midst when two or three of us are gathered together, not when we are off by ourselves.

We learn this in our families. When families work right, they are God's way of teaching us to share, work together, and care for each other. Growing up in a family helps us learn that we cannot have everything our own way. We learn to compromise and rub up against each other in ways that knock off some of our rough edges.

Living in a family can also teach us how to fight. If you grew up with brothers and sisters you know what I mean. I had both, a brother and a sister, so I had plenty of practice. I had a hard time winning a fight with my brother who was three years older than me and much bigger. But I could win one with my little sister who was almost ten years younger. One time when she and I were having a wrestling match, I held her down and said that if she didn't quit bugging me I would lick her nose. She stuck out her tongue at me, so I licked her nose. She started screaming like I had broken her arm. Mother came running and I was in trouble. But from that time on, all I had to say to my sister when she was being a pest was, "Quit that or I'll lick your nose." Years later my sister said she was so grossed out by that threat that it affected her in a negative way. Thirty years later, I apologized.

When families work the way they are supposed to, they know how to make up and forgive. But some families do not work right. Some families fight and do not make up. Silence is a rule in some families. If you have a problem, for heaven's sake, keep it to yourself because harmony is more important than truth or feelings.

Jesus says that the Christian family does not work well with silence. In the household of God, when your sister sins against you, you must go and talk to her. If that doesn't work, you must keep going back, taking others with you, doing everything in your power to get your sister back again.

Barbara Brown Taylor points out two interesting things about Jesus' advice.[1] The first is that he puts the burden on the victim, on the person that has been sinned against. It is up to the person who has been hurt to go to the person who has done the hurting. Second, Jesus seems much less interested in who is right and who is wrong than he is in getting the family back together again. It's important that we listen to each other and keep trying to mend the relationship. We shouldn't pretend that nothing has happened.

When we are fighting with someone there are several ways we can react. Some of us pretend that nothing happened. Forget the unkind words that were said or the coat that was never returned. Don't get angry. Just let it go. Ignoring it is better than a fight.

A second way we can react to conflict is giving the cold shoulder. We just avoid the person completely and never ask about what really happened between us.

A third strategy is revenge. We take every chance we get to put him down or make a joke at his expense. We think that revenge will make us feel better, but it doesn't.

When we fight in these ways we create for ourselves a kind of living hell. There is a haunting picture of hell created by the writer, C.S. Lewis.[2] It's especially alarming because it sounds too much like the place where many of us live right now. For Lewis, hell is a vast gray city inhabited only at its outer edges. It has rows and rows of empty houses in the middle. Those houses in the middle are empty because everyone who once lived there has fought with their neighbors and moved. Then they quarreled with their new neighbors and moved again. This is how hell got so enormous, says Lewis, empty at the center and inhabited only on the edges. It happened because all the people who fought with each other chose distance instead of confrontation. So hell spreads and leaves a large deserted center with people scattered around on the fringe.

Confrontation brings people face-to-face to talk things through and come to a solution. That is what this gospel recommends, and it is what many of us would do just about anything to avoid. We have lots of excuses. It was her fault, not mine. Why should I go to her? If I tell her about my hurt feelings, she'll just hurt them again. These excuses are just fine if we don't mind living on the outskirts of hell. They will not do for those of us who are called to live in Christian community. For us there is something more important than being right or wrong, and that something is keeping the family together. The problem is not the brother or sister who sins against us. The real problem is our own fierce determination to defend ourselves against them regardless of the cost.

There is another way to deal with conflict according to Jesus. We can go to the person and tell them what we think is wrong. We can even admit we might be wrong. (That's a great way to mend a fight.) Jesus urges us to do this, to do everything possible to win back a relationship that is in danger of being lost.

So go ahead and make that phone call or set up the lunch date or write the letter. If you do, you will help stop the spread of hell. If the thought of making that call scares you, don't let that stop you. There is not a word in today's reading about wanting to reach out. Just go, it says, and do everything you can to win back the relationship.

In a lot of ways it is a real bother to be a member of a family. It would be so much easier if we were just a bunch of individuals whose affairs are private, just between me and God. But here Jesus says clearly that there is no such thing as privacy in the family of God. Life together is where we come to know both each other and God.

When someone wrongs us, we are to be the first to reach out, even when we are not the guilty one, even when all we really want to do is fight back. We are called to be family, to confront and make up, to forgive and be forgiven, to heal and be healed. God is asking us to throw a block party right in the middle of the deserted center of hell and fill the place with such music and laughter that all the residents who have moved away come creeping back to the center to find out what all the joy is about. Amen.

---

1. Barbara Brown Taylor, *The Seeds of Heaven* (Cincinnati, Ohio: Forward Movement Publications, 1990), p. 58.

2. C.S. Lewis, *The Great Divorce* (New York: Macmillian, 1946), p. 16f.

Proper 19
Pentecost 17
Ordinary Time 24
Matthew 18:21-35

Throwing Away the Calculator

Then Peter came and said to him, "Lord, if another member of the church sins against me, how often should I forgive? As many as seven times?" Jesus said to him, "Not seven times, but, I tell you, seventy-seven times. For this reason the kingdom of heaven may be compared to a king who wished to settle accounts with his slaves. When he began the reckoning, one who owed him ten thousand talents was brought to him; and, as he could not pay, his lord ordered him to be sold, together with his wife and children and all his possessions, and payment to be made. So the slave fell on his knees before him, saying, 'Have patience with me, and I will pay you everything.' And out of pity for him, the lord of that slave released him and forgave him the debt. But that same slave, as he went out, came upon one of his fellow slaves who owed him a hundred denarii; and seizing him by the throat, he said, 'Pay what you owe.' Then his fellow slave fell down and pleaded with him, 'Have patience with me, and I will pay you.' But he refused; then he went and threw him into prison until he would pay the debt. When his fellow slaves saw what had happened, they were greatly distressed, and they went and reported to their lord all that had taken place. Then his lord summoned him and said to him, 'You wicked slave! I forgave you all that debt because you pleaded with me. Should you not have had mercy on your fellow slave, as I had mercy on you?' And in anger his lord handed him over to be tortured until he would pay his entire debt. So my heavenly Father will also do to every one of you, if you do not forgive your brother or sister from your heart."

If we had Bibles in the pews I would ask you to open them up now. Something remarkable is going on in Matthew

18. I'll give you a brief summary.

• Chapter 18 begins with the disciples asking Jesus who is the greatest in the kingdom of heaven. Jesus puts a child in their midst and says that anyone who becomes as humble as the child is the greatest in the kingdom of heaven.
• Second, Jesus tells the story of the shepherd who risks everything to save one lost sheep.
• Third, Jesus offers a formula for handling conflict in the church.

The common element here is that they all call upon us to throw away the calculator when dealing with relationships. No care is too great when dealing with the little ones (people who are vulnerable). No risk is too great when seeking after a lost sheep. No effort is too great when trying to restore peace in the church. Today's text tells us to throw away the calculator when it comes to forgiveness. The central issue is reconciliation. We have come full circle in Matthew 18. The chapter began by letting us know we come into the kingdom by standing in the shoes of a child. Here, at the end of the chapter, the same humility takes the shape of a slave with a debt so enormous only an act of majestic pardon can wipe it out.

The problem of the servant in today's parable is that he missed the experience of forgiveness altogether. He thought he was getting off the hook and that was the end of it. It never crossed his mind that what was really happening to him was that he was being forgiven from the heart by someone who understood how huge his debt was, but who was willing to let it all go — throwing away the calculator. You see, the debt had become a substitute for the relationship and the debt had to go if they were going to get to know each other again.

That is what real forgiveness is about. The only reason

for any of us ever to forgive each other is because we want the relationship back again. It's hard to do that when you're always keeping score and you can't seem to put away the calculator. As long as we are focused on what someone owes us, we tend to spend our time figuring out how to get paid back, proved right, or protected from more harm. But once we have forgiven our brother or sister from the heart, there is all the time in the world: time to put the calculator away and go for a walk, time to compare notes on what you have learned, time to get to know each other again.

That's what the wicked servant missed. When the king forgave him, he figured he had outsmarted the old goat and that the best way to cut his losses was to see that the same thing did not happen to him. When his turn came, he did what he had expected the king to do to him: he grabbed his debtor by the throat and demanded to be paid. He had missed his own forgiveness, so of course he could not forgive anyone else.

You know how the story ends. He gets thrown in jail until he can pay his debt, which amounts to the rest of his life, but his imprisonment is a technicality. The wicked servant was already behind bars, bars of his own making. By refusing to be forgiven and refusing to forgive, he had already created his own little Alcatraz where he sat in solitary confinement with his calculator and kept track of his accounts.

By the end of the parable, Peter thinks he has gotten the message: do unto others or the king will do unto you. Only that is not the message at all. The message of the parable is "Do unto others as the king has *already* done unto you." It's not a matter of earning your forgiveness or letting others off the hook so that you can get off the hook yourself. It is a matter of understanding that you have *already* been forgiven. There is someone who knows absolutely everything about you, all your good points and your bad ones. This someone has examined your credit rating and knows the chances for repayment are next to nil, so he took your stack of IOUs and tore them to shreds for one reason and one reason only. This someone wants to remain in relationship with you. When someone like that has stopped keeping score on you, you feel sort of foolish keeping score on the people in your own life.

How often should we forgive? Will seven times take care of it? "Not seven times," Jesus said, "but, I tell you, seventy-seven times" (v. 22). This is no burden, no job, no chore. This is a promise, because forgiveness is a way of life. What God knows and we don't yet is that once we get the hang of it, seventy times seven won't be enough, not to mention seventy-seven times. We'll be so carried away by it that we'll hope it never ends. Amen.

---

*Themes borrowed from Barbara Brown Taylor, *Seeds of Heaven* (Cincinnati: Forward Movement Publications, 1990), p. 65.

Proper 20
Pentecost 18
Ordinary Time 25
Matthew 20:1-16

To Drown Hell and Burn Heaven

> For the kingdom of heaven is like a landowner who went out early in the morning to hire laborers for his vineyard. After agreeing with the laborers for the usual daily wage, he sent them into his vineyard. When he went out about nine o'clock, he saw others standing idle in the marketplace; and he said to them, "You also go into the vineyard, and I will pay you whatever is right." So they went. When he went out again about noon and about three o'clock, he did the same. And about five o'clock he went out and found others standing around; and he said to them, "Why are you standing here idle all day?" They said to him, "Because no one has hired us." He said to them, "You also go into the vineyard." When evening came, the owner of the vineyard said to his manager, "Call the laborers and give them their pay, beginning with the last and then going to the first." When those hired about five o'clock came, each of them received the usual daily wage. Now when the first came, they thought they would receive more; but each of them also received the usual daily wage. And when they received it, they grumbled against the landowner, saying, "These last worked only one hour, and you have made them equal to us who have borne the burden of the day and the scorching heat." But he replied to one of them, "Friend, I am doing you no wrong; did you not agree with me for the usual daily wage? Take what belongs to you and go; I choose to give to this last the same as I give to you. Am I not allowed to do what I choose with what belongs to me? Or are you envious because I am generous?" So the last will be first, and the first will be last.

My dad was a good storyteller. He grew up on a farm in southern Minnesota in the days when there were no movie theaters or other kinds of entertainment, so my dad and his friends made their own fun. Judging by his stories, their entertainment involved a lot of pranks. Their imaginations really went wild at Halloween. Some of his stories I can't tell in public, but here's one I can tell. One Halloween night, my father and his friends snuck over to Uncle Ludwig's farm. They proceeded to systematically take apart Ludwig's old wooden cart, the big one he pulled behind the horses for picking corn. After they had it apart, they put the pieces in grain sacks and climbed up to the roof of the barn. Sitting way up there on top of the barn, they reassembled the cart. We kids would all collapse in giggles imagining the look on Ludwig's face when he went out to do the milking and saw his wagon on top of the barn.

People pulling tricks is one thing. We can laugh at that. But God pulling tricks is something else. In this story in Matthew it sounds as though God is pulling a very mean trick. The disciples are jockeying for the power positions in Jesus' cabinet. Jesus says the first will be last and the last first. To teach them what he means, he tells a story.

Early one morning a manager goes to the marketplace to hire some workers. He offers a handful of men a denarius each for a full days' work. They agree and head back to the vineyard. Before long, it is apparent that more workers are needed, so three more times the manager goes back to the marketplace for more workers. Finally, at 5:00 in the afternoon, with just one hour of daylight remaining, he goes back one more time. He finds another handful of men he can hire and back to the vineyard they go.

Just one hour later comes the moment they have all been waiting for — the handing out of the wages. The steward begins by going to the end of the line to the last person hired and hands him a denarius. Those at the front of the line who worked the whole day get excited thinking, "Wow! He's going to raise the amount he offered us if he's paying a whole denarius to the guys who worked just one hour." Not so. Each worker received the same pay, whether they started at dawn or lounged in the marketplace until the last hour of the day. The early workers were angry. They felt that a bad trick has been played on them. They confront the manager, who reminds them that he paid them what they agreed on. He kept his part of the bargain. What business is it of theirs to tell him how he should run his affairs? It is his money, his vineyard. Can't he do what he wants with what is his? He asks, "Do you begrudge my generosity?" You bet they do. Like most humans, they have a keen sense of what is fair and what is not. Equal pay for equal work is fair. Equal pay for unequal work is not fair. What's most interesting in this story is how the pay is received, and how it is received depends entirely on what each person believes he *deserves*.

We all know that life is not fair, which makes it seem all the more important that God should be. God should be the one authority we can count on to reward people according to their efforts. People *should* get what they deserve but according to this story, that's not how God operates.

Imagine yourself standing in line for two hours to get into a theater. You get there extra early so you can be at the front of the line. Then the manager comes out and says the end of the line comes in first. How would you feel?

How we react to Jesus' story depends on where we imagine ourselves in the line. I think most of us would imagine ourselves at the front of the line. We see ourselves as the ones who get the short end of the stick. We are the ones who are tricked and cheated out of what we deserve. I'll bet that's how 95% of us hear this story.

Did you ever consider that you might be mistaken about where you are in the line? It's entirely possible that we are halfway around the block, as far as God is concerned, with almost everyone else before us in the line. You want to cry because your chances of getting in are next to nothing. Then the manager comes out, and shock of all shocks, he beckons you in first. You and everyone at the end of the line begin to cheer and those at the front start to grumble, and you didn't do a thing to deserve this remarkable turn of events.

God is not fair. God actually seems to enjoy reversing the systems we set up to explain why God should love some of us more than others. Because God is not fair, there is a chance we will get more than we deserve, and not because of who we are, but because of who God is.

There is an image from literature that has stuck in my mind for years. The witch of Alexandria is walking around the streets of the city armed with a pitcher of water and a flaming torch. All the while she is crying out, "Would that I could drown hell with this water and burn heaven with this torch so that people would love God for himself alone." If only we could just wipe away our fear of hell and get rid of the conviction that we are earning our way into heaven. Then maybe we really could love God for who God is and let God be God.

There was a well-known trickster in Norwegian literature. His name was Peer Gynt. As a child, Peer couldn't seem to separate fact from fiction and he never stuck to anything very long. As a young man he ran off with Solveig but he soon got tired of her and abandoned her. Peer went on to have many adventures in life, but he never stands for anything and he never seems to see anything through. As an old man, Peer finds his way back to Norway. In the middle of a deep forest he pauses to eat a wild onion. As he peels away the layers of the onion, he thinks about himself and the layers of experience in his own life. Panic strikes him as he searches for the core of the onion. He realizes that his life is like the onion… layer after layer with nothing in the middle, nothing to give it meaning. His life was nothing but a long series of missed opportunities. Along comes a button molder who is looking for him. The button molder says to Peer, "You are going into my ladle."

"What will happen to me there?" asked Peer nervously.

"You will be melted down," says the button molder.

"Melted?" says Peer. "But this isn't fair. I'm sure I deserve better treatment than this. I'm not nearly as bad as you think. I've done a lot of good things. I might be a bungler, but I'm not an awful sinner either."

"That's just the problem," said the button molder, "that's why you're going into the ladle. You're not one thing or the other."

In a panic Peer asked, "What should I do? How can I learn to be myself?"

The button molder answered, "Stand forth everywhere with the Master's intention displayed like a signboard." Peer was devastated. He had failed. He had never wondered what he was supposed to be. He cried out for one last chance to prove that he was somebody and that he had an identity.

He ran to the hut of Solveig, the girl he had left behind so many years ago. Peer called for her to curse him, because leaving her was a terrible thing for him to do. The button molder waited at the side of the house to hear her reply. Peer was stunned when Solveig hugged him with joy. "You have made all my life as beautiful as a song," she exclaimed. "Blessed are you for returning."

Peer pleaded with her, "Ask me where I have been all these years."

Solveig smiled. "Oh, that riddle is easy."

Peer urged her again. "Then tell me what you know! Who am I? Where was I, as myself, as the whole man, the true man? Where was I?"

Solveig replied, "In my faith, in my hope, and in my love. That's where you were."

Peer's face lit up as he realized that he **had** been somebody. He was somebody in Solveig's heart! He **had** had an identity in her love all that time as she waited and longed for him.

Peer Gynt cried out, "In your love... oh there hide me, hide me!" The button molder disappeared into the distance.[1]

It's a good thing God isn't fair. We just might get more than we deserve. We might even realize one day that we have been hidden in God's love for a whole lifetime while we labored with him in the vineyard. Amen.

---

1. The story of Peer Gynt taken from Michael Rogness, *The Hand That Holds Me* (Minneapolis: Augsburg Publishing House, 1984), p. 42.

Alternative Sermon for

Proper 20
Pentecost 18
Ordinary Time 25
Matthew 20:1-16

Being Too Generous

For the kingdom of heaven is like a landowner who went out early in the morning to hire laborers for his vineyard. After agreeing with the laborers for the usual daily wage, he sent them into his vineyard. When he went out about nine o'clock, he saw others standing idle in the marketplace; and he said to them, "You also go into the vineyard, and I will pay you whatever is right." So they went. When he went out again about noon and about three o'clock, he did the same. And about five o'clock he went out and found others standing around; and he said to them, "Why are you standing here idle all day?" They said to him, "Because no one has hired us." He said to them, "You also go into the vineyard." When evening came, the owner of the vineyard said to his manager, "Call the laborers and give them their pay, beginning with the last and then going to the first." When those hired about five o'clock came, each of them received the usual daily wage. Now when the first came, they thought they would receive more; but each of them also received the usual daily wage. And when they received it, they grumbled against the landowner, saying, "These last worked only one hour, and you have made them equal to us who have borne the burden of the day and the scorching heat." But he replied to one of them, "Friend, I am doing you no wrong; did you not agree with me for the usual daily wage? Take what belongs to you and go; I choose to give to this last the same as I give to you. Am I not allowed to do what I choose with what belongs to me? Or are you envious because I am generous?" So the last will be first, and the first will be last.

Dan and I always enjoyed the summer days at the lake cabin in Minnesota. It's a noisy and happy time with grandchildren running around in wet bathing suits, adults scooping ice cream like crazy, playing our favorite game Double Cross, and swatting mosquitoes. Late in the evening we would start telling stories. Sometimes we laugh until we cry. At some point in the storytelling, our oldest child usually says to her siblings, "You don't know how lucky you were. Our parents were so strict with me I couldn't come in even ten minutes late. You owe me big time for breaking them in." We all laugh, but I also feel some good Lutheran guilt. Dan and I *have* been unfair. We were unfair when we spent so many hours with the child who was getting into trouble. It wasn't that we loved the well-adjusted children any less. Spending many more hours with the struggling child was simply our way of showing love. But yes, it was not fair.

The parable of the laborers in the vineyard presents us with a similar situation. It's a strange story. We don't know why the landowner would go out to the marketplace five times a day, including just one hour before the work day ends. We don't know why he brings in all the workers he can find and doesn't seem to be interested in choosing the strongest or smartest. Why does he do the work of hiring when he could have sent his manager? Then, at the end of the day, he does an even stranger thing. He gives the same wage to every worker, regardless of whether the worker started at daybreak or noon or one hour before quitting time. This is clearly a different kind of landowner. The parable is a little like cod liver oil. You know Jesus is right. You know it must be good for you, but that doesn't make it any easier to swallow.

We think that the way to win God's attention is to be the first one into the vineyard in the morning and the last one to leave at night. According to this parable, that will get us exactly nowhere in the kingdom of God. Not only will the ones who came last get the same pay as those who worked all day, but they get paid first. It turns out that the landowner knows exactly what he's doing when he tells the manager to give out the pay to the last workers first. He could have made the situation easier by paying the workers in the order in which they had arrived. Then those first workers would have gotten their pay and gone home without knowing that the later workers were paid the same. But this is central to the story. The first workers are made to see that the last workers are paid the same. Why? What are those first workers supposed to acknowledge and the rest of us understand?

To answer the question it helps to check out what comes before and after the parable. Immediately before, Peter has asked Jesus what he and the others can expect to receive for their loyalty to him. Right after our parable, James' and John's mother asks Jesus to make her sons his president and vice president. The parable comes between two situations where Jesus' own disciples are jockeying for position in the kingdom. In addition there's the formula that comes before the parable and after: "So the last will be first and the first will be last." For some of us that is good news. Let's say you waited in a line outside the movie theater for a whole hour. Then the manager comes out and says, "Okay, folks. Those of you at the end of the line are going in first." You would be mad. It isn't fair. But for the people at the end of the line it would be good news. Here's the point: if God is not fair, then there is a chance that some of us will get paid more than we deserve. For reasons we may never understand, God seems to love us indiscriminately. God rearranges all the systems we set up to explain why God should love some of us more than others.

According to the story, the landowner just feels like being generous. That's all. He can do whatever he wants. It is his vineyard, after all, and what he wants is to let the last be first and the first be last. Everyone will be paid. No one will go home empty handed. He simply wants to reverse the order and pay everyone the same regardless of how long they have stood in the sun. The owner asks the workers, "Do you begrudge my generosity?" The answer is, "You bet we do." We should get what we deserve, we say.

I love the wisdom of the desert fathers. They were humble, uncomfortably honest, and their wisdom has a different twist to it. There is a story about one of the brothers to whom the devil keeps appearing. One night, the devil came to him disguised as an angel of light. The angel said to him, "I am the Angel Gabriel, and I have been sent to you." But the brother replied, "Think again. You must have been sent to someone else. I haven't done anything to deserve an angel." Immediately the devil stopped appearing to him.

When it comes to the kingdom of God, I — for one — am happy I don't get what I deserve. What I deserve is to be left standing at the end of the line forever. But that's not what I get. Instead, those of us who came first and worked hard all day are invited to join the owner in welcoming those who came last, and to do this without comparing or complaining. Why not celebrate? In this kingdom, no matter which group you are in, everyone ends up with more than they deserve. Amen.

Proper 21
Pentecost 19
Ordinary Time 26
Matthew 21:23-32

The Gift of Failure

When he entered the temple, the chief priests and the elders of the people came to him as he was teaching, and said, "By what authority are you doing these things, and who gave you this authority?" Jesus said to them, "I will also ask you one question; if you tell me the answer, then I will also tell you by what authority I do these things. Did the baptism of John come from heaven, or was it of human origin?" And they argued with one another, "If we say, 'From heaven,' he will say to us, 'Why then did you not believe him?' But if we say, 'Of human origin,' we are afraid of the crowd; for all regard John as a prophet." So they answered Jesus, "We do not know." And he said to them, "Neither will I tell you by what authority I am doing these things. What do you think? A man had two sons; he went to the first and said, 'Son, go and work in the vineyard today.' He answered, 'I will not'; but later he changed his mind and went. The father went to the second and said the same; and he answered, 'I go, sir'; but he did not go. Which of the two did the will of his father?" They said, "The first." Jesus said to them, "Truly I tell you, the tax collectors and the prostitutes are going into the kingdom of God ahead of you. For John came to you in the way of righteousness and you did not believe him, but the tax collectors and the prostitutes believed him; and even after you saw it, you did not change your minds and believe him."

When I was an eighth grader, there was a day that was so painful I still remember it clearly. I was to give a speech about New York in an English class. I was so nervous, I decided to try my speech out on a group of friends the day before. My fear made me cocky. I delivered the whole speech to my friends calling the city Yew Nork and acting like a clown. You can guess what happened. During my speech the next day, every time I said New York I stumbled. I just couldn't get the words out. The more I stumbled the more nervous I got. The students were laughing and the teacher was mad. It was awful. I was a dismal failure.

But that failure taught me something. I never acted like a show-off again, no matter how nervous I was. Failure had turned out to be an odd kind of gift. Now that everyone in that class knew the worst I could do, there was nowhere to go but up!

Jesus tells another parable. This one is about a father and two sons. The father tells the first son to go and work in the vineyard. The son says sure and then doesn't go. The father tells the second son to go and that one says no, but then later goes. Then Jesus asks the religious leaders, "Which of the sons did the will of the father?" They say the second son of course. Jesus says to them, "*You* are the son that did not go, because you chose not to go into God's vineyard, tax collectors and prostitutes are going into the kingdom of God before you." Imagine their shock. It's like saying an ex-con will get into the kingdom before a church council member. (Remember, Jesus is speaking to leaders of the synagogue.) The point of the parable is this: Everything depends on going into the vineyard and doing God's work. God is looking for people who will go, and according to the Bible, a person who has failed is more likely to respond.

Let's put the parable into a more modern form. There was a family living in Spring Hill that had two sons. The first son succeeded in everything. He was an *A* student in high school. He was taking post-secondary classes and getting *A*s in those too. He was a champion debater, a great football player, and a Merit Scholar. He knew he was good. Things just came easy for him. The second son was different. He struggled with almost everything. He had a learning disability, so classes were hard. He was barely passing. Then he got caught smoking in the boy's bathroom and was labeled a troublemaker. He skipped school from time to time and made some other poor choices. The second son felt like a failure. It happened that the father of these sons had been collecting books to take to the nursing home down the street. So the father went to his first son, the super achiever, and asked him to take a box of books to the nursing home. The son said sure, but he never intended to do it. He went off to practice with his debate partner instead. The father asked the second son to do the job, and he said no. He was watching a football game on television, but later he relented and went.

Barbara Brown Taylor said, "Wisdom is not gained by *knowing* what is right. Wisdom is gained by *practicing* what is right, and noticing what happens when that practice succeeds and when it fails."[1] God needs people who will answer the call to work in his vineyard. We don't have to be trained teachers or organizers. We don't even have to be certain about what we believe. We certainly don't need to be a success. We need to go — to practice what is right. The Bible says that the vineyard was filled with failures. So you're a failure? Fine.

Jacob was a failure. In another story of two sons, Jacob stole the inheritance from his brother Esau by deceiving their father, Isaac. As a result, Jacob had to run for his life. Years later he returned home to face his brother. Jacob was worried. He didn't know how Esau would react when he saw him, so Jacob camped overnight at the River Jabbock while he worked up his courage. In the middle of the night he had a wrestling match with a stranger. Just when Jacob thought he might be was winning, the man reached out, touched Jacob's thigh, and his hip was thrown out of joint. Jacob knew he was defeated. In pain he knew he could not win. So he grabbed hold of the stranger, hung on for dear life, and demanded a blessing. The angel-stranger blessed him. But this time Jacob doesn't get the blessing by being sneaky. This blessing he receives in pain is a blessing he can only receive as a gift.

Being a failure doesn't necessarily mean that we will listen to God and work in the vineyard. Failure just might teach us that we cannot make it on our own. Abraham learned that. Abraham failed over and over again, but he went when God called. Moses too. Moses was an impatient man and a poor public speaker but he led the people of Israel out of slavery. And Jacob… Jacob, must have really looked like a failure when he went limping home to ask his brother's forgiveness. Jesus, too, was regarded as a failure. Jesus of Nazareth staggered on bleeding feet toward the cross. Then he stumbled forth from the tomb, lurching toward the resurrection, bearing on his body the signs of the defeat that was victory for all. The world would call all of these people failures. However, they had something very important in common. They knew they needed God. Failure didn't matter because they knew God would be with them in the vineyard. Think of what we could do if we *all* knew that. Amen.

---

1. Barbara Brown Taylor, *An Altar in the World* (New York: HarperOne, 2009), p. 14.

Proper 22
Pentecost 20
Ordinary Time 27
Matthew 21:33-46

Divine Tenants

Listen to another parable. There was a landowner who planted a vineyard, put a fence around it, dug a wine press in it, and built a watchtower. Then he leased it to tenants and went to another country. When the harvest time had come, he sent his slaves to the tenants to collect his produce. But the tenants seized his slaves and beat one, killed another, and stoned another. Again he sent other slaves, more than the first; and they treated them in the same way. Finally he sent his son to them, saying, "They will respect my son." But when the tenants saw the son, they said to themselves, "This is the heir; come, let us kill him and get his inheritance." So they seized him, threw him out of the vineyard, and killed him. Now when the owner of the vineyard comes, what will he do to those tenants? They said to him, "He will put those wretches to a miserable death, and lease the vineyard to other tenants who will give him the produce at the harvest time." Jesus said to them, "Have you never read in the scriptures: 'The stone that the builders rejected has become the cornerstone; this was the Lord's doing, and it is amazing in our eyes'? Therefore I tell you, the kingdom of God will be taken away from you and given to a people that produces the fruits of the kingdom. The one who falls on this stone will be broken to pieces; and it will crush anyone on whom it falls." When the chief priests and the Pharisees heard his parables, they realized that he was speaking about them. They wanted to arrest him, but they feared the crowds, because they regarded him as a prophet.

My husband's first call as a pastor was to a small parish in North Carolina. The parsonage was on a large corner lot.

The hill in the backyard was badly eroded with wide grooves running down to a little creek. Shortly after we moved in I learned that the US Forestry Service would give away 100 pine seedlings to anyone who would use them for soil conservation. I ordered the seedlings and went out one fine spring day to start planting pine trees. I was on my hands and knees planting seedlings when a neighbor came over to see what I was up to. After I explained what I was doing, he said, "Well, I guess it makes sense... except that you don't own the house."

That was true. We didn't own the house. We didn't own much of anything. We had a few pieces of furniture, fifteen boxes of books, and several thousand dollars worth of student loans. Many of us start out that way, poor and renters. If we go back far enough, most of us can claim ancestors who were hired help working someone else's land. In the south they called them sharecroppers and in the west, migrant workers. Elsewhere there were tenant farmers or homesteaders. Many of our grandparents and great-grandparents didn't own anything to speak of, much less land. Two years before I planted those seedlings in North Carolina, I visited the old family farm in Norway. It stood on a hillside in a beautiful and rugged valley that looked as though it grew more rocks than crops. The people were poor and rugged too, but they were strong and friendly. All of the people in that little valley had our two family names. But the 500-year-old family farm had a different name. Suddenly I realized why. My relatives were all poor. They had never owned that farm. They had tended someone else's land, brought in someone else's crops, and made a profit for someone else.

Barbara Brown Taylor points out that this is not the American way. The American way is to own your own home on your own land, growing your own crops, and tending your own vegetable garden. Most of us in this country believe in ownership and independence. These are the values we have been taught and these are the values we strive to live by.

If we believe Jesus' parable, however, those are not the values of the kingdom. Ownership of the vineyard is not the issue. This vineyard is not for sale and never will be. The owner isn't looking for buyers, he is looking for tenants, people who will give him his share of the crops at harvest time. This parable is about stewardship and that's a word that sticks in our craw. We would much rather talk about ownership.

You and I have worked hard for what we have. We have deeds, titles, fences, and hedges to prove our ownership. We have gone to a lot of trouble to get these things and we are proud of them. But, according to the parable, we are fooling ourselves. Our ancestors became divine tenants so long ago that we have forgotten where it happened or when. Somewhere along the way someone lost the tenant's agreement and wrote up a deed instead. The landowner spent most of his time in another country, you see, so it didn't seem to matter. When he finally sent messengers to remind the tenants of their agreement, they responded with violence and the messengers ran away. The owner could have sent the police or retaliated in some other way, but he did not. He just kept sending the messengers, each one pleading with the tenants to come to their senses and honor the agreement they have with the owner of the land.

Finally, when the cemetery is overflowing with dead messengers, the owner sends his son. The son came alone and unarmed hoping to teach the tenants something they had forgotten. He reminded them that ownership was a game they had made up. He told them that it was good to be tenants because tenants don't have to worry about responsibilities they can't handle. As tenants they had free access to more than they ever could have earned for themselves. Being a tenant is a good thing he said. It's like being a guest because it puts them in relationship with the owner and with each other. Once they quit playing the ownership game, their relationship can be based on gratitude, not competition so everything necessary for life could be shared. All the son asked was that they take care of the vineyard and give him a portion of what they produced. The son didn't need it, of course. He turned right around and gave it away to others because they needed it. The tenants needed to give in order to remember who they were: grateful guests who received their lives like the gifts they were and turned around and gave themselves to others.

The tenants killed the son too but he would not stay dead. To this day he is still haunting the vineyard, reminding us that we are God's guests. We are welcome to everything on the earth as long as we remember who it belongs to and how to care for it. We can love all of it as our own and water the flowers and plant the trees to stop erosion and enjoy the harvest. What we cannot do is ignore the owner or his messengers. That would be inviting disaster because it would mean we have forgotten who we are and where we have come from. We are God's tenant farmers. We care for the earth on behalf of someone else. We represent God's interests, being as generous with each other as God is with us. We are not owners. We were never meant to be. This is *not* the American way, but it is the way of the kingdom and when the harvest finally comes, well, it will take your breath away. Amen.

---

*Themes borrowed from Barbara Brown Taylor, *Gospel Medicine* (Boston: Cowley Publications, 1995), p. 96.

Alternative Sermon for

Proper 22
Pentecost 20
Ordinary Time 27
Matthew 21:33-46

Captains or Parties

Listen to another parable. There was a landowner who planted a vineyard, put a fence around it, dug a wine press in it, and built a watchtower. Then he leased it to tenants and went to another country. When the harvest time had come, he sent his slaves to the tenants to collect his produce. But the tenants seized his slaves and beat one, killed another, and stoned another. Again he sent other slaves, more than the first; and they treated them in the same way. Finally he sent his son to them, saying, "They will respect my son." But when the tenants saw the son, they said to themselves, "This is the heir; come, let us kill him and get his inheritance." So they seized him, threw him out of the vineyard, and killed him. Now when the owner of the vineyard comes, what will he do to those tenants? They said to him, "He will put those wretches to a miserable death, and lease the vineyard to other tenants who will give him the produce at the harvest time." Jesus said to them, "Have you never read in the scriptures: 'The stone that the builders rejected has become the cornerstone; this was the Lord's doing, and it is amazing in our eyes'? Therefore I tell you, the kingdom of God will be taken away from you and given to a people that produces the fruits of the kingdom. The one who falls on this stone will be broken to pieces; and it will crush anyone on whom it falls." When the chief priests and the Pharisees heard his parables, they realized that he was speaking about them. They wanted to arrest him, but they feared the crowds, because they regarded him as a prophet.

My father was not a particularly pessimistic person, but I remember one conversation we had that sure sounded like he was. I was a teenager and thinking out loud about what I might like to do with my life. My father was being the realist. I said maybe I would like to be a doctor. He said it took eight years of education after high school and we didn't have the money. I said, well maybe I will be a missionary to Africa. He said I would die from some awful, rare disease. Then I said I might like to be a soloist with the Metropolitan Opera. He said there were probably thousands standing in line waiting to audition for a single opening. Finally, I said in frustration, well, I guess I'll be a farmer then. Dad said nobody can afford to buy a farm these days. I gave up.

I thought of that conversation with my dad when my young son came to tell me he was taking a *Des Moines Register* paper route. I asked, "Do you realize what you're getting into? You will be going to bed at night before your favorite TV shows just so you get up when it's dark out and deliver papers when it's raining or snowing or 20 degrees below zero. Plus you have to do the bookkeeping to keep track of what people pay and owe." My son argued with me about every point I made. Then it hit me. I was making the same mistake my father had made twenty years earlier. It's no fun to take a good hard look at ourselves and see that we are the problem.

This parable Jesus tells us is like that. It's easy for us to point our fingers at the tenants and call them evil. They were, after all. If we really want to understand the story we have to see ourselves in it and that hurts. The owner of the vineyard is God. The owner's son is Jesus. The tenants are the religious leaders, and they are us. Like Pogo said, "We have seen the enemy and they is us."

The tenants' mistake is that they want to keep that which has only been lent to them. They were terrible people. They killed the boss' messengers and then the son. The parable implies we are like this. If we put ourselves into the story, then we have to ask, "Do we take from God that which belongs to God and put it in our pockets? Do we treat God as miserably as those tenants did?" I hate to say it, but I guess we do.

For example, we tend to identify ourselves with our nice things. We brag about our cars. We are proud of our houses. We pat ourselves on the back for having a good brain or a big bank account. We identify with our possessions.

On the other hand, we push aside everything that incriminates us. We blame our parents for our shortcomings or our friends or our sensitive emotional makeup. Ultimately we even blame God for some of the bad things in our lives.

In our story, the tenants claim everything as their own, even though they are simply renting. They pride themselves on their ability to work, the fruit they produce, and even the vineyard itself. They are like the poem "Invictus" written by William Henley:

> It matters not how strait the gate,
> How charged with punishments the scroll,
> I am the master of my fate:
> I am the captain of my soul.[1]

When we make ourselves into captains and give ourselves credit for all we have accomplished, we avoid having to depend on God. According to the story, this is not the way to live.

So how does God intend for us to live? Perhaps we have a hint in the Law of Moses. Once a year, at the time of Passover, all Jewish families brought to the temple one tenth of all they possessed. Not simply one tenth of their annual income, but one tenth of all they owned. These gifts were not used for maintaining outreach programs or supporting the priests in the temple. This vast accumulation of wealth was used for a party! Can you believe it? A party! All the people of Israel were expected to travel to Jerusalem and participate in a gigantic blow-out party. And everyone was invited: the tax collector, the poor, the rich, the lame, and the blind! No wonder the children of Israel said, "I was glad when they said to me, 'Let us go to the house of the Lord!' " (Psalm 122:1).

In ancient Israel, God was worshiped in celebration. The kingdom of God is more like a party than a soup kitchen. So, if God loves a party, then those who refuse to party in God's name lose out on the glory of the kingdom.

One important thing for us to remember is that there are limitations to partying. Moses taught that one tenth of our assets in any one year must be set aside for partying. The other nine tenths are to be used in service to others in God's name.

Our lifestyles should give evidence that we are happy, party-going disciples of the one who invites us to the magnificent banquet. But sacrifices are to be made for the poor. Unfortunately, most of us have turned God's formula around. We spend nine tenths of what we possess on the party while the remaining tenth goes for service in the kingdom. This gives us a new perspective on being the captains of our souls and rejecting the son of the landlord. The problem is that we cannot get away from our own greatness. We've twisted the image of God that we carry into a social-climbing, money-hoarding tenant who kills the messenger and finally the son himself rather than give up our dependence on ourselves and our own greatness. We've got the party routine backward.

Jesus came to make it possible for us to celebrate and live for others. He knows us. He sees that we reject him and that we prefer our own selfish goals. Yet he keeps coming, keeps offering his alternative way. Either we remain the captains of our souls and reject the son, or we let God be the captain and become God's party-people living upside-down lives of joy and generosity. All of life will not be a party, of course, but when the rough patches come, at least we will know that the real captain is right there beside us. Why would anyone choose something else? Amen.

---

1. William Ernest Henley, "Invictus," *Masterpieces of Religious Verse*; ed: James Morrison (New York and London: Harper and Brothers Pub., 1948), p. 575.

Proper 23
Pentecost 21
Ordinary Time 28
Matthew 22:1-14

Wedding Guests

Once more Jesus spoke to them in parables, saying: "The kingdom of heaven may be compared to a king who gave a wedding banquet for his son. He sent his slaves to call those who had been invited to the wedding banquet, but they would not come. Again he sent other slaves, saying, 'Tell those who have been invited: Look, I have prepared my dinner, my oxen and my fat calves have been slaughtered, and everything is ready; come to the wedding banquet.' But they made light of it and went away, one to his farm, another to his business, while the rest seized his slaves, mistreated them, and killed them. The king was enraged. He sent his troops, destroyed those murderers, and burned their city. Then he said to his slaves, 'The wedding is ready, but those invited were not worthy. Go therefore into the main streets, and invite everyone you find to the wedding banquet.' Those slaves went out into the streets and gathered all whom they found, both good and bad; so the wedding hall was filled with guests. But when the king came in to see the guests, he noticed a man there who was not wearing a wedding robe, and he said to him, 'Friend, how did you get in here without a wedding robe?' And he was speechless. Then the king said to the attendants, 'Bind him hand and foot, and throw him into the outer darkness, where there will be weeping and gnashing of teeth.' For many are called, but few are chosen."

When I was a college student, I would sometimes bring a friend home for a weekend. I always had to warn the friend that my dad was a practical joker. Once when we were all sitting at the dinner table, my dad passed the butter plate to my boyfriend. As my friend put out his hand to receive it, my dad gave the plate an extra shove and my friend ended up with his thumb stuck in the soft butter. My dad laughed like crazy. I wanted to cry. My friend just sat there looking at a glob of butter on his thumb. Another time, Daniel, my future husband, was with us, wearing a favorite old shirt. There were some little holes in the back of it. My dad put his finger in one of the holes and ripped the shirt all the way to the bottom. Dan was shocked! Not me. I knew that if you were a guest at our house, you had to have a sense of humor or you were sunk.

Today, Jesus tells a story about guests but these guests are guests in the kingdom of God. To understand the story, it helps to know that the early church had a discipline problem on their hands. Some believers bellied up to God's table with no sense of what it meant to be there. As far as they were concerned, it was a come-as-you-are party, because Jesus had squared everything with God. So then everyone was welcome and nothing was required: no dressy clothing, no special table manners, no RSVP.

Wrong! Totally wrong, according to Matthew. Being an invited guest to the kingdom party does not mean you may do as you please. Even being invited at the last minute does not mean anything goes. Matthew says, "People, you have been invited to feast with the king. Now, rise to the occasion and be the king's people!"

Like everything else in the story, the wedding robe has a deeper meaning. It is not a white linen tunic embroidered with gold thread. It is a whole way of life — one that honors the king, one that recognizes the privilege of being called into his presence, even if the invitation arrives at the last minute. The underdressed guest's mistake was not that he showed up in shorts and sandals. It was that he showed up too full of himself and thought no one would notice, least of all the king.

On the one hand, this is a story addressing a particular

situation in the life of the early church and no longer has anything to do with us. On the other hand, it happens every Sunday right here. This worship service may not be the heavenly wedding banquet, but it is certainly the rehearsal dinner, where each of us gets to practice our parts. Everyone was invited to be here this morning but as you can see, some of us had other things to do. Some are on the golf course. Some are at work. Some are still in bed. But we are here, and not necessarily because we are better than they are. Like the underdressed guest, some of us have rolled in here without thinking much about it. We showed up with our spiritual shirttails hanging out, lining up at the buffet table as if no one could see the ways in which we have refused to change and adapt to the desires of the king. Some of us have refused to surrender our fears and resentments. Some have refused to share their wealth. Some have refused to respect the dignity of every human being. These are the old clothes we wear to the king's banquet. These are the clothes we prefer to the wedding robe of new life, and these old clothes are as painful to the king as a bride dressed in black.

We make the same mistake as the underdressed guest who thought the king was just looking for warm bodies at his banquet. He was happy to eat the king's food and enjoy the king's music if that's what the king wants. But it isn't. God is not looking for warm bodies. God is looking for wedding guests, who will rise to the occasion of honoring the son. We can do that in shorts and sandals as well as in suits and high heels. Wedding garments are not made out of denim or silk, you see. They are made from the whole fabric of our lives using the patterns God has given us: patterns of justice, forgiveness, compassion, generosity, and peace. When we wear those clothes, we are gorgeous in the sight of the king. Absolutely gorgeous.

To wear a wedding garment is to know the significance of the occasion, to allow God's gracious invitation to change us and live accordingly. Here's a story of what the change might look like.

Some of you will remember George Eliot's story of Silas Marner. Silas was an unlikable old miser. He was falsely accused of stealing. So he lived fifteen bitter years as a recluse. His only interest in life was to take out his pile of gold at night and let the shining pieces run through his fingers. One night that too was stolen from him by a burglar. His life was shattered. Then one New Year's Eve a poor, homeless woman left her little blonde daughter sleeping in front of the fireplace in Silas' cottage. The next day, Silas found the mother's dead body.

Nobody claimed the child, so she lived as a guest of Silas the miser. Slowly the old man fell under the spell of the wonderfully cheerful child. The delight of caring for her gradually caused him to forget his lost gold. As she grew and moved cheerfully among the villagers, Silas too was drawn from his shell and began to speak to his neighbors. The cottage took on a new appearance. Lacy curtains decorated the once-shuttered windows. Silas was happy. There was light in his eyes, a smile on his face, affection in his voice, and a bounce to his step. He was no longer a hermit turned in on himself. The focus of his life had shifted to the little girl and then to his neighbors. His life had been transformed by a guest.

The kingdom of God does not come about simply by giving in to a royal command. The kingdom comes when something happens in the heart of the guest, then the joy of the king becomes the joy of the guest, and the mission of the king becomes the mission of the guest. So put on your wedding garment of justice and peace, generosity and compassion. Then you'll be ready whenever the invitation arrives. And you'll want to be ready, because this is a party not to be missed. There'll never be another one like it. Amen.

If You Like This Book...

Kristin Borsgard Wee has also written the Pentecost-First Third section titled "Do You Love Me?" for *Sermons on the Gospel Readings*, Series III, Cycle B (978-0-7880-2544-0) (printed book $37.95, e-book $22.77); and *Formed By a Dream*: First Lesson, Pentecost-Last Third, Cycle A (978-0-7880-1819-0) (printed book $8.95, e-book $7.61).

contact
CSS Publishing Company, Inc.
www.csspub.com
800-241-4056

Prices are subject to change without notice.

www.ingramcontent.com/pod-product-compliance
Lightning Source LLC
Chambersburg PA
CBHW071757040426
42446CB00012B/2596